Taking Turns

By Janine Amos and Annabel Spenceley

Consultant Rachael Underwood

CHERRYTREE BOOKS

A CHERRYTREE BOOK

This edition first published in 2007
by Cherrytree Books, part of
The Evans Publishing Group Limited
2a Portman Mansions
Chiltern Street
London W1U 6NR

Printed in China

Amos, Janine

Taking turns. - Rev. ed. - (Growing up)
1. Social participation - Pictorial works - Juvenile
literature 2. Social interaction - Pictorial works -
Juvenile literature
I. Title
302.1'4

ISBN 9781842344927

CREDITS
Editor: Louise John
Designer: D.R.ink
Photography: Gareth Boden
Production: Jenny Mulvanny

Based on the original edition of Taking Turns published in 1997

With thanks to: Jack Hetherington, Reuben Rosso, Bryony Jones, Tayce Rickets and Danielle Rutter.

Bike Ride

Danielle is on the bike.

Tayce wants it.

Tayce pushes Danielle off
and takes the bike.

How do you think Tayce feels?
How do you think Danielle feels?

Danielle feels sad and angry.

What do you think will happen next?

Danielle grabs the bike back.

Danielle and Tayce shout.

Danielle's mum comes over.
"Danielle, you look upset,"
says Mum.

"And Tayce, you seem angry."

"I want the bike!" says Tayce.

"I was on the bike. You pushed me," says Danielle.

Danielle and Tayce both want the bike. What could they do?

"Tayce can have the bike when I've finished my go," says Danielle.

"I'll ride round three times," says Danielle. "Then it's your go."

"OK," agrees Tayce.
"I'll count."

They have worked it out. Danielle's having a turn on the bike.

Now it is Tayce's turn.

They have both had a turn.
How is Danielle feeling now?
How is Tayce feeling?

On the Slide

Reuben is on the slide. He is going down on his tummy.

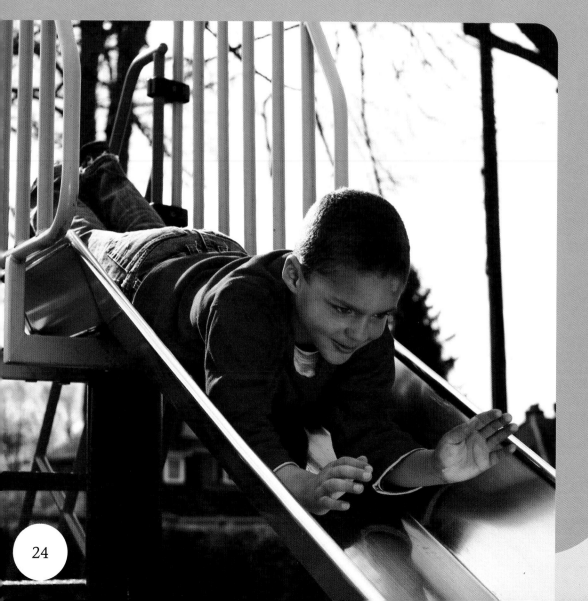

Jack wants to slide, too.
"Hurry up!" calls Jack.
**What do you think will
happen next?**

Jack sets off. Reuben is
still on the slide.

They crash!

"That hurt me!" says Reuben.
"It hurt me, too!" said Jack.

What could they do next time to solve the problem?

Next time
Reuben waves
when he has
finished his turn.

And Jack waits
until Reuben is
off the slide.

31

Teachers' Notes

The following extension activities will assist teachers in delivering aspects of the PSHE and Citizenship Framework as well as aspects of the Healthy Schools criteria.

Specific areas supported are:

- Framework for PSHE&C 1b, 1c, 1e, 2a, 2e, 2h, 4a, 4b, 4d, 5b, 5f
- National Healthy School Criteria 1.1, 4.3

Activity for *Bike Ride*

You will need a one-minute timer and a box of snap together blocks/bricks.

- With the children sitting in a circle ask for 6 volunteers. Choose your 6 and ask them to come to the middle.
- Tell everyone that the task is for the 6 children together to build the longest line of bricks they can in one minute. If the line breaks at any point all the joined bricks must be discarded and a new line started!
- Start the timer and allow the children to try. Let them work however they choose to – only intervene if absolutely necessary.
- At the end of the minute ask each of the 6 children if they thought it was fair. What went wrong?
- Tell the children you want to read them a story about two girls who both wanted to do the same thing at the same time.
- Read the *Bike Ride* story.
- At the end of the story ask all the children if there was anything that happened in the story that reminded them of the children doing the task with bricks.
- What solution for the brick group could they suggest?
- Invite the 6 children to return and build their line again only this time using the suggestions from the group about taking turns.
- Ask all the children to notice what happened the second time.
- Ask the six participating children how it felt this time. Which time did they prefer? Which method produced the longest line? Which method involved everybody fairly?

Activity for *On the Slide*

Read the story to the children.

- With the children sitting in a circle ask them if they have ever had an accident or been hurt when they were playing with someone.
- After each child has told their story ask them and the wider group what they could have done differently in order to have played safely. For example they could have slowed down, waited until the way was clear, kept further away, taken turns etc.
- Explain that we always have to make choices when we play and sometimes we can't help it if we get hurt unless we choose not to play at all. Everyone falls over sometimes. But sometimes we can make choices to keep us from getting hurt like taking turns, not doing dangerous things like walking on high walls or climbing on high things.
- Ask each child to draw a picture for a poster telling children how to play safely. Cut out the pictures and mount them on a large sheet of paper with captions and advice from the children. Label the poster 'Playing Safely'.